Rookie
Biographies®

Amelia Earhart

by Wil Mara

Content Consultant
Nanci R. Vargus, Ed.D.
Professor Emeritus, University of Indianapolis

Reading Consultant
Jeanne M. Clidas, Ph.D.
Reading Specialist

Children's Press®
An Imprint of Scholastic Inc.
New York Toronto London Auckland Sydney
Mexico City New Delhi Hong Kong
Danbury, Connecticut

Library of Congress Cataloging-in-Publication Data
Mara, Wil.
 Amelia Earhart/by Wil Mara; content consultant, Nanci R. Vargus, Ed.D., professor
emeritus, University of Indianapolis; reading consultant, Jeanne Clidas, Ph.D.
    pages cm. — (Rookie biographies)
  Includes index.
  ISBN 978-0-531-21059-8 (library binding) — ISBN 978-0-531-24980-2 (pbk.)
1. Earhart, Amelia, 1897-1937—Juvenile literature. 2. Air pilots—United States—
Biography—Juvenile literature. 3. Women air pilots—United States—Biography—
Juvenile literature. I. Title.

 TL540.E3M333 2014
 629.13092—dc23[B]   2013034808

Produced by Spooky Cheetah Press
Poem by Jodie Shepherd
Design by Keith Plechaty

Photographs © 2014: Ames Historical Society/Courtesy of Farwell T. Brown
Photographic Archive/Ames Public Library: 15; AP Images: 23, 24, 27, 31 center
top; Corbis Images: 12 (Hulton-Deutsch Collection), 11 (Underwood & Underwood);
Getty Images: 8 (FPG), 4, 31 center bottom; Newscom/Everett Collection: 19;
Shutterstock, Inc./Brian A Jackson: 3 top; Superstock, Inc./Everett Collection: 28, 30
right; The Image Works: 16, 30 left (Scherl/SZ Photo), 20, 31 bottom (Topham), cover
(Underwood Archives); Thinkstock: 3 bottom (Hemera), 31 top (iStockphoto).

Maps by XNR Productions, Inc.

Table of Contents

Meet Amelia Earhart

Amelia Earhart changed the world by breaking the rules. When she was a child, there were no female pilots. Amelia did not let that stop her from becoming one of the first. She is an inspiration to young women around the world.

Amelia showed that a woman can do anything a man can.

Amelia was born in Atchison, Kansas.

Amelia was born in Atchison, Kansas, on July 24, 1897. Amelia did not like to play the types of games most girls played. She liked to do things that boys usually did. She and her younger sister, Grace, were raised to believe that they could do anything boys could do.

FAST FACT!

Amelia enjoyed doing what she called "first-time things." For her entire life, she loved the thrill of trying something new.

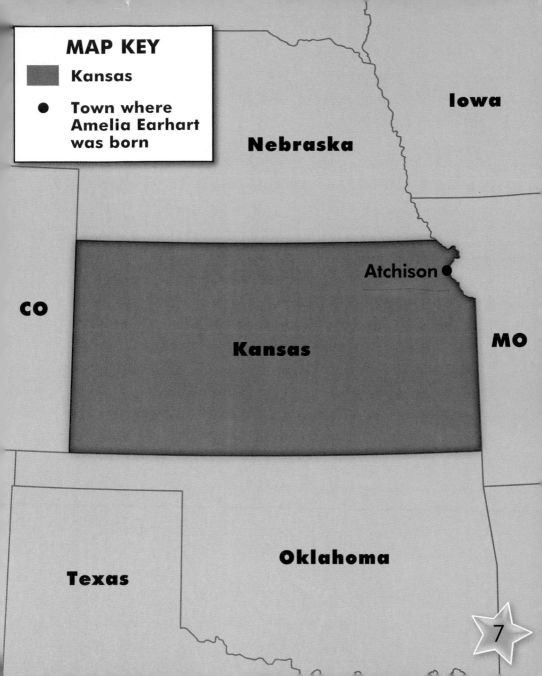

MAP KEY

Kansas

● Town where Amelia Earhart was born

Iowa

Nebraska

CO

Atchison ●

Kansas

MO

Oklahoma

Texas

8

A Young Adventurer

Amelia and Grace liked to go on pretend adventures. They dreamed of traveling to faraway places. As Amelia grew up, many of her heroes were women who dared to go into jobs that men usually held. She collected newspaper articles about them.

Amelia was about three years old when this photo was taken. Her sister was one.

After her high school graduation, Amelia visited her sister in Canada. While she was there, Amelia saw wounded soldiers returning from World War I. She quickly decided that "doing good" was more important than going to school. Amelia became a nurse's aide.

This is Amelia's high school graduation photo.

After a year in Canada, Amelia went to live with her parents in California. When she and her father attended an air show, Amelia took her first ride in an airplane. She was hooked! Amelia knew she wanted to become a pilot.

When Amelia went to her first air show, not many people had flown in or even seen an airplane.

13

Flying High

Amelia began taking flying lessons less than a month later. Her instructor was a woman named Neta Snook. Very few women had a pilot's license at this time, but that did not bother Amelia. She earned her license on May 15, 1923. She was one of the first women ever to do so!

Like Ameila, Neta Snook was one of the first female pilots.

14

Wilmer Stultz (left) was the pilot who flew Amelia across the Atlantic.

Flying was fairly new—and very dangerous—when Amelia got her license. In 1927, a pilot named Charles Lindbergh became the first person to fly across the Atlantic Ocean. Many others had tried it and died. In 1928, Amelia got the chance to make the trip, but only as a passenger.

In 1929, Amelia married George Putnam.

Amelia's flight made her famous, and she put her fame to good use. She spent a lot of time talking to women about how they could pursue their dreams, too.

FAST FACT!

In November 1929, Amelia helped start a club for women pilots. It was called the Ninety-Nines. The name came from the number of women who attended the club's first meeting.

20

In May 1932, Amelia got a chance to fly across the Atlantic Ocean again. Only this time she would be flying the plane herself! Another woman had already tried and failed. But Amelia was successful.

In 1935, Amelia broke another **record**. She became the first person to fly alone across the Pacific Ocean.

A crowd gathered to meet Amelia after her flight across the Atlantic.

Her Final Flight

In 1936, Amelia decided to try flying around the world. Other pilots had done it before, but Amelia wanted to be the first to follow the **equator**. That is the invisible line that circles the widest part of the Earth. It would take a full year to plan the trip.

In this photo, Amelia and her navigator plot their route on a map.

Amelia needed to know exactly how much fuel she would need. She also needed to figure out when and where she would have to stop to get more. For this trip, Amelia took along **navigator** Fred Noonan. A navigator's job is to figure out what route a pilot will take on a journey.

This is a photo of Amelia and Fred Noonan.

By July, Amelia's journey was
almost over. Then something went
very wrong. On July 2, Amelia
was scheduled to stop at Howland
Island in the Pacific Ocean. She
never arrived. People searched
for Amelia and Fred, but they were
never seen again.

FAST FACT!

Amelia's disappearance is a mystery. No
one knows where—or why—she crashed.
Even today, teams are actively looking
for the wreckage of her lost plane.

Timeline of Amelia Earhart's Life

1897
born in Atchison, Kansas

1920
takes first plane ride

1923
receives pilot's license

Amelia Earhart never gave up on her dream. She did not care that most pilots were men. She broke many records and won many awards. Today Amelia is remembered as a **pioneer**.

1932
becomes first woman to fly across the Atlantic Ocean alone

1937
disappears while trying to fly around the world

1929
marries George Putnam

1935
becomes first person to fly solo across the Pacific Ocean

29

A Poem About Amelia Earhart

At a time when most women stayed at home,

Amelia had the urge to roam.

She took to the skies and learned to soar,

going places no woman had gone before.

You Can Be a Pioneer

- When you do something, give it your all. Try to do it better than anyone else.

- Do not be afraid to try new things—even if they seem out of your reach.

- Stay focused on your dreams. Do not let anyone get you off course.

Glossary

equator (i-KWAY-tur): imaginary line around the middle of the Earth

navigator (NAV-u-gay-tor): a person who uses maps and compasses to guide a pilot

pioneer (pye-uh-NEER): one of the first people to work in a new and unknown area

record (REH-kerd): the greatest achievement in a certain field

Index

Facts for Now

Visit this Scholastic Web site for more information on Amelia Earhart:
www.factsfornow.scholastic.com
Enter the keywords **Amelia Earhart**

About the Author

Wil Mara is the award-winning author of over 140 books. Many are educational titles for children.